CHRISTIAN
PERFECTION

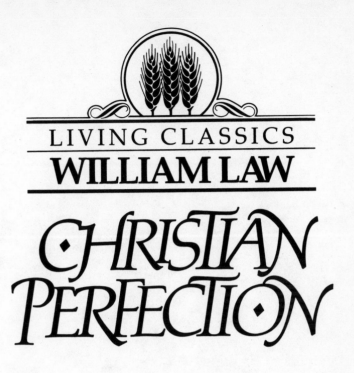

LIVING CLASSICS
WILLIAM LAW

CHRISTIAN PERFECTION

A Contemporary Version by
Marvin D. Hinten

Tyndale House Publishers, Inc.
Wheaton, Illinois

William Law's original work was first published
in 1726 under the title *A Practical Treatise Upon
Christian Perfection.*

The Scripture quotations are from *The Bible in
Today's English Version.* Copyright © American
Bible Society, 1966, 1971, 1976.

First printing, March 1986
Library of Congress Catalog Card Number 85-51985
ISBN 0-8423-0259-X

CONTENTS

THE LIFE OF WILLIAM LAW

William Law was born in England in 1686. After attending Emmanuel College, Cambridge, he was ordained as an Anglican clergyman in 1711 and continued at Cambridge with a fellowship. In 1716 he was forced to leave both the ministry and the university for refusing to take the oaths of allegiance to George I, the new king and head of the Church of England.

Edward Gibbon, grandfather of the author of *The Decline and Fall of the Roman Empire*, hired Law in 1723 as a tutor for his son (the historian's father). During that time, Law produced his two greatest works—*On Christian Perfection* (1726) and *A Serious Call to a Devout and Holy Life* (1729).

In 1740 he left the Gibbon household and retired to King's Cliffe—his birthplace—where he had inherited a small property from his father. Law devoted himself to prayer and good works until his death in 1761.

INTRODUCTION

William Law's *A Practical Treatise Upon Christian Perfection* (1726) indicates by its title Law's hope for the book. He wanted it to be practical. And to Law, the most practical thing a book can do is lead us to try to please God. In his other great classic, *A Serious Call to a Devout and Holy Life*, Law describes one character this way: "She cannot resist buying practical books. (By practical, naturally, she means books on holiness and the Christian life.)"

For scores of years *Christian Perfection* was practical in just that way. Dr. Samuel Johnson, the eighteenth-century author and critic, called it the "finest piece of hortatory theology in any language." But words like *hortatory* have passed from our vocabulary, and the nuggets of spiritual gold in *Christian Perfection* have been buried under two-and-a-half centuries of language change.

Now the gold is again at the surface. This modernized and abridged edition provides the essence of *Christian Perfection*. It is spiritually practical for contemporary devotion. Not only is the diction updated, but so are the examples. Law's original versioin spoke of the Christian's need to avoid steamy stage plays, while this abridged version speaks of time-wasting soap operas and frothy sex comedies. But only the illustrations and diction are modernized; in condensing and paraphrasing William Law's thoughts, I have not substituted my own.

There are elements in *Christian Perfection* with which we may disagree. But the book encourages us to take God seriously and to try to please him. Thus do we fulfill God's will. As Law says in Chapter 8, "God is perfectly reasonable. He therefore only wills that his reasonable creatures be more reasonable and perfect—more like himself."

—Marvin D: Hinten

CHAPTER ONE
THE NATURE
OF CHRISTIANITY

PERFECTION may seem to imply some state that not everyone needs to aspire after, a degree of holiness not practical for most Christians. But by perfection I mean simply holy conduct in every condition of life.

I call it perfection for two reasons. First, I hope it fully represents the holiness and purity to which Christianity calls all of us. Second, it's an inviting title.

To rightly perform our duties and to have holy attitudes is not only the highest degree of Christian perfection; it is also the lowest the gospel allows. None of us, pastor or layman, can go higher; none of us can securely rest any lower.

To illustrate, let us consider one particular aspect of Christianity, our love for God. Christians are to love God with all their heart and all their strength. Who can go further than this? But who can aim lower—that is, who can be excused from fulfilling this command?

What is true for loving God is true of our other duties. The yearning after Christian perfection is necessary for all Christians. As there is but one faith and one baptism, there is but one holiness, a holiness which all should strive for.

Someone may object that not all people can be equally good, just as not all people can be equally wise. That's true in one sense and false in another. For instance, if we consider charity as giving money to the poor, all people cannot be equally charitable, since some have much more to give away than others. But if we consider charity to be a charitable frame of mind, all people may be equally charitable. The charitable frame of mind is an aspect of Christian perfection.

As to our performance of Christian duties, there may be a great difference. One person may engage in many business dealings and be honest in them all; another may be honest in his few dealings. If they both have honest minds, they are equally honest, though one is able to exhibit his honesty much more often.

A person cannot exercise martyrdom till he is brought to the stake. He cannot forgive his enemies till they have done him wrong. He cannot bear patiently with poverty and distress until they come upon him. So, obviously, some acts of virtue depend on outward circumstances. But any person may have a spirit equal to those circumstances if they occur. A person who has no one to forgive is not considered hard-hearted, and a person who has no wealth to give away is not considered uncharitable. We are not all in distress, but we can all have thankful hearts prepared for distress. So people can differ in instances of goodness and yet be equally good.

There may also be differences in action founded in our differing abilities. One person may be wiser than another and see more clearly into Christianity, practicing it more effectively, while another is not so wise, yet practices his Christianity as best he can. Goodness consists in being faithful to what we know. If a person is faithful to the knowledge God has given him, he is as good as someone faithful to greater light. We can hardly reconcile it with God's goodness for one man to have five talents and another only two unless we believe that God is as pleased with the right use of two talents as of five.

Everyone is called to goodness and perfection; no one has ever fully achieved it. In spite of his giving the command of perfection, God in his mercy admits to happiness people who have not been perfect. If God did not pardon our frailties and failures, even the best men could not be rewarded. But consider now: Does God's pardon of failure prove we are not called to perfection? Does God's forgiveness of defects in our goodness mean we are not called to be good? Surely not.

Someone might claim that people can be saved without trying for the perfection to which they were called. But though people will be admitted to heaven without reaching perfection, it does not follow that people will be admitted to heaven without *striving* for perfection. There is surely a great difference between falling short of perfection and stopping short of it.

You say you will be content with simply believing and being saved? That is foolish reasoning. God gives rewards; men don't take them. No one should say, "I will practice just so much Christianity, and then take my heavenly reward." The yearning for perfection should be present in everyone, and everyone should desire to use his abilities to the utmost.

God sees different abilities and weaknesses in each person, and in his goodness he shows mercy to different levels of holiness. I grant that some people with very little holiness may be accepted by God. But consider: Though weak holiness may be accepted by God, it cannot be chosen by us. We are not living a holy life if we *choose* to be weak. God may be merciful to small holiness because of pitiable circumstances. But when we choose small holiness, it becomes great unholiness. This book, then, is about our necessary efforts toward perfection, our striving for holiness.

CHAPTER TWO
WHO ARE WE?

WHO are we? Why are we placed on earth? These questions have been asked by wise men through the ages. Human misery and the impermanence of enjoyments make it difficult for wise men to discover the source of happiness.

God has satisfied our inquiries by revealing to the world his Son, Jesus Christ. This revealing has opened his great secrets; it has given us all the information necessary to calm our anxieties and lead us safely to happiness. All we must do is not exalt our own poor wisdom against God. We simply allow our eyes to be opened by him who made them, and let our lives be conducted by him in whom we live and move and have our being (Acts 17:28).

There is now light in the world, if we are willing to come out of the darkness. This light has acquainted us with God. It has added heaven to earth and eternity to time, giving us a peace that passes understanding.

The revealing of Jesus Christ acquaints us with these facts: We have a spirit within us, created after the divine image. This spirit is now in a corrupt condition, enslaved to fleshly thoughts within a body-tomb. Blinded with false notions of good and evil, our spirits do not remember the taste of true happiness.

Christ's revelation further teaches that our world is also disordered and cursed. It is not the Paradise God created, but the remains of a drowned world, full of sin and the marks of God's displeasure. It is a wilderness where dreams and shadows sometimes please, sometimes agitate, and sometimes torment our short, miserable lives. Devils reside here, promoting darkness and seeking whom they may devour.

Man's natural condition, then, is like a person sick from several diseases. Knowing neither his illnesses nor their cures, he is enclosed in a place where everything he sees or tastes continually inflames his diseases.

Christianity puts an end to this. The entire purpose of Christianity is to lead us from all thoughts of rest and satisfaction here, to deliver us from the slavery of our own natures and unite us to God, the fountain of all real good. It does not leave us to cast about for worldly happiness but prepares us for the enjoyment of a divine life.

"I am the way, the truth, and the life," says our blessed Savior. "No one goes to the Father except by me" (John 14:6). Just as everything was first created by the Son of God, so are all things restored by the same person. Just as nothing could come into being without Christ, nothing can enter a state of happiness with God without Christ.

The price of our redemption both confounds our pride and relieves our misery. How fallen we must be from God to need so great a Redeemer! On the other hand, how precious we must be that so tremendous a means should be taken to restore us to God's favor.

All the teachings of the gospel are founded on these two great truths: the corruption of human nature and its new birth in Christ Jesus. One explains all our misery; the other contains all our hope of happiness. On these doctrines the whole frame of Christianity is built. Christianity forbids only things that fasten us to sin and commands only those duties which lead us into the liberty of the children of God.

Our corrupt nature makes self-denial and bodily death necessary. Our new birth makes the sacraments and the reception of God's Spirit necessary.

To know our true condition we must search after a life that is hidden with Christ in God (Col. 3:3). We pity efforts at human greatness when we see a corpse lying in state. But if Christianity were to form our judgments, the life of a sensual person, though that person might be renowned, would cause us just as much pity. As the apostle said, one who lives in pleasure is dead while one lives (1 Tim. 5:6). Thus our lives must be more than enjoyment and pleasure, which are often the signs of living men and dead Christians. Therefore, to know what is good for us, we must look at nothing temporary. We might as well dig in the earth for wisdom as look at worldly enjoyments to find out what we want.

You will see every person in the world pursuing his imaginary happiness, but when you see this you are seeing the world asleep, chasing after dreams. If you wish, you may go to sleep. You may lie down and dream, for that is as happy as the world can make you. But it is like sleeping in a ship when you should be pumping out the water.

Suppose some being should try to please you by describing how fine a place to live the sun is. He describes its brightness and mineral riches and tells you it is a peaceful place. Would you not think it a sufficient answer to say, "I am not meant to live there"?

When your human nature is trying to please itself with

worldly joys and desires, is it not an equally good answer to say to yourself, "I am not meant to stay here"? For what is the difference between happiness on the sun to which you can never go and earthly happiness from which you are to be eternally separated?

Consider the littleness of human honors. In the Book of Esther, the great king Xerxes asked Haman, his chief minister, "What shall be done for the man whom the king wishes to honor?"

Haman, imagining he was the man, answered, "Have royal robes brought for this man—robes that you yourself wear. Have a royal ornament put on your own horse. Then have one of your highest noblemen dress the man in these robes and lead him, mounted on the horse, through the city square. Have the noblemen announce as they go: 'See how the king rewards a man he wishes to honor' " (Esther 6:7-9).

Here you see the insignificance of worldly honor. An ambitious Haman cannot think of anything greater to ask. Every man can see the littleness of all rewards—except those which he is trying to get for himself.

We ridicule countries in which people bury shoes and money with the corpse to help it in the afterlife. Yet if we understood life truly, we could as easily ridicule our living efforts. We may buy finer houses, put on nicer clothes, eat out more often, get more entertainment, and these will help us to be finally happy as much as shoes will help a dead man walk.

You don't think yourself talked out of any real happiness when you are persuaded not to be as ambitious as Alexander the Great. Conversely, you should not think yourself drawn away from real happiness by being persuaded to be as contented as Jesus.

CHAPTER THREE
NEW BIRTH

CHRISTIANITY is not just a school for teaching better morals or polishing our manners. It is deeper—it implies an entire change of life.

What does it mean to be "born of God"? According to John, "Whoever is a child of God does not continue to sin" (1 John 3:9). This doesn't mean that anyone born of God is flawless and cannot fall into sin. It means that whoever is born of God is possessed with the idea of avoiding sin; he labors to keep from it.

One might say of a miser that "he sure doesn't spend his money." This doesn't mean he *never* spends money, but that he labors against spending, and expenses are contrary to his intention. An expense troubles him, and he returns to saving with extra diligence. Similarly, a person born of God intends only purity and holiness; in that sense, he does not commit sin. We attempt to avoid sin as a miser avoids expense. We are not Christians unless we are born of God. We are not born of God unless we (in this sense) do not commit sins.

Also, whoever is born of God loves. Christ said, "Love your enemies and pray for those who persecute you, so that you may become sons of your Father in heaven" (Matt. 5:44, 45). There is perhaps no duty of Christianity more contrary to our natural selves. We cannot exercise this duty until we are entirely changed.

Our Savior said, "Whoever does not receive the Kingdom of God like a child will never enter it" (Luke 18:17). The change from infancy to adulthood is great; surely the change from adulthood to infancy is at least as great.

Infants have everything to learn; they must be taught by others what to hope for and fear. In this sense we are to become infants, being taught what to choose and what to avoid.

And if the new life is like birth, the old life is like death. Paul says, "For you have died, and your life is hidden with Christ in God" (Col. 3:3). Our old self dies when we become Christians. Paul says in another letter, "For surely you know that when we were baptized into union with Jesus Christ, we were baptized into union with his death. By our baptism, then, we were buried with him and shared his death" (Rom. 6:3, 4). So baptism is not just a rite through which we enter the church, but a consecration which presents us as an offering to God, just as Christ was offered at his death. Baptism does not make us Christians unless it brings us into death and consecrates us to God.

We are to copy Christ. The Savior purchased humanity with his blood, not to live in ease and enjoyment, but to drink of his cup, to be baptized with the baptism he underwent, and like him to be perfected through suffering. Again Paul says, "All I want is to know Christ and to experience the power of his resurrection, to share in his sufferings and become like him in his death" (Phil. 3:10). Redemption came by sacrifice, and the redeemed conform to it.

Many people are content with outward decency—moral behavior with an old heart. A person need not be a Christian, however, to be fair. A heathen can be temperate. To make these virtues part of Christianity, we must have them proceed from a new heart. A Christian should be honest for the same reasons and with the same spirit that he takes Communion. Just as eating bread and drinking wine are of no spiritual use without the proper frame of mind, so our other religious duties are empty and meaningless unless our minds and hearts are renewed.

Some people, when becoming Christians, believe that living the Christian life means "doing what church people do." So a man notices church people don't smoke, and he stops smoking. Or a woman notices that church people attend worship services, so she attends. But Christianity is not practicing a particular virtue, or seeing how few vices we can manifest, but letting God control our attitudes.

People think they have sufficiently reformed if they are different in some particular way. But it is a mistake to be contented with ourselves because we are less vain or more kind than we used to be. Those who measure themselves by themselves are not wise (2 Cor. 10:12). Christ is the only standard by which we should measure ourselves.

Only spiritual rebirth assures salvation. As the Scripture says, "When anyone is joined to Christ, he is a new being" (2 Cor. 5:17). All other attainments are insignificant, as Christ showed: "When the Judgment Day comes, many will say to me, 'Lord, Lord! In your name we spoke God's message, by your name we drove out demons and performed many miracles!' Then I will say to them, 'I never knew you' " (Matt. 7:22, 23).

So let us examine our spirits, and not consider ourselves safe because we act respectable and belong to the "right" church. If not all those who prophesy in Christ's name belong to him, surely not all those belong to him who are merely baptized in his name.

CHAPTER FOUR
WORLD, FLESH, AND DEVIL

CHRISTIANITY ranks the world as an equal enemy with fleshly desires and the Devil. God indulged the Jews in worldly hopes and fears, giving them a land on this earth to possess. The gospel is different; "My kingdom does not belong to this world," our Savior said (John 18:36).

Further, he said, "None of you can be my disciple unless he gives up everything he has" (Luke 14:33). Even the lawful concerns of this world can render us unfit for Christianity. Serious businessmen generally look down on idlers. But a person who centers his heart on being a successful businessman is as unattractive to God as any other self-gratifier. What difference does it make whether a man ignores God in an office or a casino?

Worldly cares are no more virtuous than worldly pleasures; Christ calls us from both. It is a mistake to give our hearts to either.

I will agree that nature makes some cares, such as making a living, necessary. The same is true of some pleasures—eating, drinking, rest. But Christianity must control both the cares and the pleasures.

Some say our Savior's teaching about forsaking everything relates only to the first Christians. I agree that Christianity finds different circumstances in different ages. But though the external state of the church changes, Christ's teaching about the internal state of Christians does not change.

The world may sometimes favor Christianity and other times persecute it. This makes no difference in the need for personal holiness. Such attributes as humility, longing for heaven, devotion, love, and renunciation of the world are always to be part of the Christian life.

So we must examine carefully to what the first Christians were called. If they were called to suffer at the hands of other people, that may (perhaps) not be our case. But if we find them called to suffer from themselves, in voluntary self-denial, we can hardly limit that calling to the first century. Why would the kingdom of heaven require heavenly affection and worldly disregard in the first century, but make no demands on our own time?

Let us see what Scripture requires of Christians regarding the world. Mark tells us, "As Jesus was starting on his way again, a man ran up, knelt before him, and asked him, 'Good Teacher, what must I do to receive eternal life?' 'Why do you call me good?' Jesus asked him. 'No one is good except God alone. You know the commandments: "Do not commit murder; do not commit adultery; do not steal; do not accuse anyone falsely; do not cheat; respect your father and mother." ' 'Teacher,' the man said, 'ever since I was young, I have obeyed all these commandments.' Jesus looked straight at him with love and said, 'You need only one thing. Go and sell all you have and give the money to the poor, and you will have riches in heaven; then come and follow me' " (Mark 10:17-21).

In Matthew it is added, "If you want to be perfect, go

and sell all you have and give the money to the poor" (Matt. 19:21). Some imagine that Christ's expression "if you want to be perfect" means some uncommon perfection, a goal not meant for every Christian. The young man's question, however, plainly shows what he is aiming at; he wants to inherit eternal life.

It seems plain, then, that Jesus' command was not meant to achieve some extraordinary height, but was a condition of being a Christian and securing eternal life. For Jesus goes on to say, "How hard it will be for rich people to enter the Kingdom of God" (Mark 10:23).

Obviously, what was expected of this young man is expected of all rich men. For how would it be difficult for them if they did not have to give up their money? If they could keep their money and still enter the kingdom, the difficulty vanishes. The disciples clearly understood the difficulty, for they asked, "Who then can be saved?" Jesus answered, "With God all things are possible," implying that it is possible for God to effect this great change in people's hearts.

Some people might still imagine this command ("sell all you have") to apply only to the rich young ruler, and not to all people of wealth. But observe this young man's virtue. He was so eager after eternal life that he *ran* to Jesus, and put the question to him on his *knees*, and for these things the account says Jesus *loved* him.

Can it be imagined that Jesus would make salvation extra hard for one desiring it so? Would he impose especially hard terms on one who had already gained his love? Would Jesus hinder this young man's salvation for a reason that others might ignore? Would Jesus send him away sorrowful on terms that would be eased after his lifetime, in a later generation? Jesus did not give the command to show his authority of demanding what he pleased, but to reveal an attitude necessary for Christianity.

If Jesus felt he was offering the rich young ruler a reasonable proposal, that proposal must be equally reasonable for us.

CHAPTER FIVE
PEARL-SEEKING

"THE kingdom of heaven," Jesus said, "is like this. A man is looking for fine pearls, and when he finds one that is unusually fine, he goes and sells everything he has, and buys that pearl" (Matt. 13:45, 46). When Jesus calls the kingdom of God a fine, valuable pearl, I take him to mean that a great deal is to be given for it. When he says the man sold all that he had to buy it, I take that to mean the pearl cannot be bought for less.

Modern people want much easier terms than those of our Savior's day. In proclaiming the kingdom, we often tell them they need not sell *all* for this pearl. And we too often say that after buying it they may go on seeking other pearls as they used to do and yet be members of the kingdom of God.

The peaceful, pleasurable enjoyment of wealth is continually condemned by our Savior. "How terrible for you who are full now; you will go hungry!" (Luke 6:25). This hardly sounds as though prosperity and plenty are approved enjoyments for Christians. "But how terrible for you who are rich now; you have had your easy life!" (Luke

6:24). Woe is not threatened only to those who have enriched themselves by evil means, but to all who have taken consolation in wealth.

Some say that the story of the rich young ruler simply means we must sell our goods when they interfere with our religion; until that takes place, we may peacefully enjoy them. (One might as well say we need not resist the Devil unless he interferes with our church attendance.) From where does this interpretation come? Jesus did not say, "You may some day find it necessary to sell." His command to the rich young man was "Go *now* and sell."

Does Jesus' command mean a person must literally sell everything and give it all to the poor to inherit eternal life? I understand Jesus to forbid self-indulgence from the estate. The rich young ruler should not use his wealth for ease (as the rich man in the parable of Lazarus did), but should offer it to God for the relief of others. Selling all is a specific way of expressing that general duty.

If Christ had told sinners they had to repent in sackcloth and ashes, I would take the sackcloth and ashes to be a specific way of expressing the general duty; though the particular circumstance of sackcloth and ashes might be omitted, yet the thing intended, humiliation and sorrow, was always to be performed to the same degree. When Jesus related the Good Samaritan's charity and told his hearer, "You go and do the same," the listener was not to wait for an opportunity of doing the exact same action. He was simply to do the same *type* of thing.

Likewise, a man need not literally sell all he has to obey Jesus' command to the ruler. But it is necessary to comply with the principle intended, disregard for wealth. He sufficiently parts with his money who parts with the self-enjoyment of it and uses it to support others who lack it. To literally sell one's estate is no more necessary for renunciation of wealth than sackcloth is always necessary for true repentance.

Many people prefer to believe the literal sense of selling all, for they can thereby consider themselves excused from doing so. But if they would consider that the thing required is disclaiming self-enjoyment of wealth, they would find themselves concerned.

I appeal to your imagination. Suppose you were to observe well-to-do Christians enjoying their money, creating continual sources of entertainment, living in the best neighborhoods. Then suppose you observed Jesus, with no place to lay his head. He promises a treasure in heaven to those who will give up all for his sake. He proclaims woe to the rich and full. Now judge reasonably from your imaginings. Would you suspect these well-to-do Christians to be followers of that Lord?

Suppose someone were to send up this prayer to God. "Lord, I, your sinful creature, born again in Christ Jesus, beg you to give me more money than I need. Enable me to gratify myself and my family in the delights of entertainment, fine eating, and a fashionable neighborhood. Grant that as life goes on I may continually become better off financially. Help me to perceive the surest ways of growing richer. This I humbly and fervently beg in Jesus' name. Amen."

The same attitude that makes an unchristian prayer makes an unchristian life. The way we live is our real prayer, for as Christ said, "For your heart will always be where your riches are" (Matt. 6:21). Our heart continually prays what our life acts. We would condemn a person who prayed a prayer like that, but would call Christian the life that matches it. There is perhaps no better way of judging our affections than to see whether we can in our prayers ask God to bless our main desires.

CHAPTER SIX
RICH MAN, POOR MAN

DOES anyone think he is entitled to more pleasure for being wealthy? One might as well say a poor person, because he lacks certain possessions, is entitled to be a thief.

Why aren't poor Christians allowed to be impatient or complaining? Isn't it because Christianity requires the same virtues in every condition? Isn't it because Christ can satisfy us in every condition?

But the same reason could be given against self-indulgence by those who can afford it. A rich man who uses his money for pleasure is like a poor man who spends his time complaining. If Jesus Christ can make us rejoice in tribulation and be thankful in hardship, surely he can help us forbear luxury.

Some people say that wealth and poverty are neutral states in themselves; they are made good or evil by the inward attitudes of the ones in those states. This belief overlooks the fact that rich people *choose* to be rich. Thus their outward position reflects their inward desires. (I will admit that a poor person might be greedy. But he has not *chosen* poverty.)

So to say that a person who chooses to live in wealth has a "treasure in heaven" attitude inwardly is like saying a person who constantly fights has a peaceable attitude inside. One might as well say the town drunk has a good inner attitude toward soberness.

Christians are to love God with all our hearts, with all our souls, and with all our minds. A person who has his heart and head taken up with worldly concerns can no more love God with all his heart and mind than a person with his eyes on the ground could look straight up to heaven.

To love God wholeheartedly, we must be convinced that our only happiness is in him alone. We cannot believe this until we renounce all other efforts at happiness. If we look to God to supply half our happiness, we can only love him with half our hearts.

One might say that wholehearted love for God is impossible. Even should we grant this to be so, we must not therefore stop the effort, but imitate heavenly love as far as human nature allows.

To defend a lack of affection for God, people sometimes claim that we cannot control our emotions. Some people who love God will, because of their background or nature, not feel as close to him.

This is partly true. Our emotions are indeed influenced by our natures. But differences in our natures cannot justify a lack of desire for God. Two gluttons, by their natures, may approach and eat a batch of cookies differently. The ill-mannered one may stuff his face, while the well-mannered one eats one at a time. But desire for cookies is the controlling thought in each of them. One person may, because of his nature, be less emotional toward God than another; but the same desire rules them both.

All people desire what they believe will make them

happy. If a person is not full of desire for God, we can only conclude that he is engaged with another happiness. It's hard to love God wholeheartedly; we all know that. So why do we not remove as many hindrances as possible?

The person who recognizes that the world will not make him happy will find his heart at liberty to aspire after God. He will understand what the psalmist means: "I thirst for you, the living God. When can I go and worship in your presence?" (Ps. 42:2). Until we have that desire, we are acting Christianity without feeling it, just as a stage actor makes an angry speech without feeling angry himself.

If our hopes for happiness depend on other people, our attitudes will depend on them. We will love and hate other people to the degree that they hinder or help our happiness. We can never act otherwise until we are governed by a happiness which others can neither cause nor prevent. When we live in this state, we will not find it troublesome to love our neighbors as ourselves. It will be no harder than wishing them enjoyment of the same air and sunlight we enjoy.

Almost all Christians place some hope of happiness in the world. We need not go to evil people; let us visit any good religious family, and we will find kowtowing and coldnesses and cutting remarks, all founded on worldly reasons.

These proceed from the typical Christian attitude. Busily looking after our earthly interests, we intend only to keep clear of dishonesty and scandal. This is using the world as a virtuous pagan does, and it develops good pagan attitudes. But not just cheating and lawbreaking are harmful. The bare desire for worldly things—and placing happiness in them—lays the foundation for unchristian attitudes.

Why do most people find it so easy to love and forgive

a person on his deathbed? Isn't it because all reason for dislike or hurt feelings ceases then? All worldly interests being at an end, worldly attitudes die with them. This shows us it is necessary to die to the world if we are to live and love as Christians.

Some people think dying to the world means we must enter a monastery; but this is no more true than avoiding vanity in dress means to stop wearing clothes. We can eat reasonably, we can drink reasonably, and we can use the world reasonably. We may work, we may buy and sell, we may provide for our families—*if* we do those things within the bounds of necessity.

Some people excuse their excessive labor as family provision, saying they want to express love by leaving their children an inheritance. So, you love your children and want to see them rich. Jesus loved the rich young ruler and told him to sell all. We have Jesus' express command to love one another as he has loved us. Are you following this love when you leave to your children what Jesus commanded his beloved friend to give away to the poor? If you really love your children, you will teach them that heavenly affection is the only hope for happiness.

CHAPTER SEVEN
SUFFERING

THE foundation of Christianity is that humanity was restored by Jesus Christ's death on the cross. As Christ was holy and accepted suffering, we ought to conform to his holiness and acceptance of suffering. Christ was sinless; we should flee sin. Christ suffered; we should be ready to face suffering.

If Christ had lacked either holiness or suffering, his sacrifice would have been incomplete. We cannot expect God to accept suffering without holiness; it seems reasonable there will be no holiness without suffering.

Some people might believe that we will not need to undergo suffering, since Christ's atonement took care of the suffering our sin inevitably results in. We do not, it is true, suffer to make his sacrifice more complete or add further value to his atonement. However, it would be foolish to think that since Christ is our righteousness, we need not try to be righteous ourselves. Similarly, his suffering for our sin does not mean we will not suffer ourselves.

It's plain that Christ's suffering has not removed all other suffering for sin. Surely death is a suffering for sin—and all Christians undergo death.

Christ's suffering took place on the cross. Our suffering takes place on our own crosses in the form of self-denial. As Jesus said, "If anyone wants to come with me, he must forget himself, carry his cross, and follow me. For whoever wants to save his own life will lose it; but whoever loses his life for my sake will find it" (Matt. 16:24, 25).

We are very careful to observe baptism because our Savior instituted it. We should be equally careful to observe self-denial.

We deny ourselves to keep from being tempted by a life of ease and comfort. Therefore we can engage only in pleasures that do not make us comfortable with temptation.

Christ said, "Happy are those who mourn; God will comfort them!" (Matt. 5:4). This clearly refers not to mourning about a particular circumstance, but to a state of godly sorrow. One property of mourning is absence from entertainment. When a person begins to relish diversions and amusements again, we sense the period of mourning is near an end.

Most Christians agree that Christianity includes self-denial. But we understand self-denial in such a loose, general way that we fail to apply it to our lives.

Consider this instance from the Sermon on the Mount. "You have heard that it was said, 'An eye for an eye and a tooth for a tooth.' But now I tell you: do not take revenge on someone who wrongs you. If someone slaps you on the right cheek, let him slap your left cheek too. And if someone takes you to court to sue you for your shirt, let him have your coat as well. And if one of the occupation troops forces you to carry his pack one mile, carry it two miles" (Matt. 5:38-41).

We are to deny ourselves in not demanding a tooth for a tooth. We are to deny ourselves by exposing our cheek and suffering pain, pain which we could prevent by resistance. We are to deny ourselves by not defending ourselves in lawsuits. We must take up the cross of one injury after another, rather than contending at a trial. (Instead of securing our shirts in the lawsuit, we expose our coats to loss as well.) Anyone who would argue that we need not really accept injustice must argue that we need not really love our enemies, Christ's next command.

Some people claim Christ meant only that we are not to prosecute others. But this text does not concern a spiteful prosecution; it forbids a seemingly reasonable defensive lawsuit. Malice per se was already forbidden to the Jews of Jesus' day; but we are to go so far as to deny ourselves self-defense and justice. Many Christians think we may defend our rights if the law will support us. But Christian standards of meekness are not to be formed by human laws any more than our devotion to God is to be formed by human standards.

By personal power or legal contention we could perhaps repel injuries. But by defending ourselves, we raise our passions and embitter our tempers.

Meekness and self-denial suit the spirit of Christianity. Christians are to have forsaken all, to be dead to the world, to be as meek and lowly as Jesus. Pride, self-love, and human wisdom argue against such meekness and self-denial. But let all Christians remember what Jesus said at the close of his words on self-denial: "If a person is ashamed of me and of my teaching in this godless and wicked day, then the Son of Man will be ashamed of him when he comes in the glory of his Father with the holy angels" (Mark 8:38).

People may pretend what they please about an "inner love" while they are resisting harm or engaging in lawsuits. But Christian love is to be like the love of Christ, who died for his enemies. It must be a different kind of love that allows us to fight them. To say that you can love your enemy while in a lawsuit against him is like saying you can love your enemy while dueling with him.

A person who oppresses us offends against justice; but if we resist, we offend against meekness. And suffering can teach us obedience. The Scripture says of Christ, "But even though he was God's Son, he learned through his sufferings to be obedient" (Heb. 5:8). Now if God's only begotten Son, without sin, full of divine knowledge, received instruction from suffering, how much more must we need that learning!

To believe that we can know about obedience to God without suffering is to say we do not need the help the Son of God had. Sufferings ought to be considered among God's grace.

The same Letter to the Hebrews earlier says that Jesus was "crowned with honor and glory because of the death he suffered" and he was made "perfect through suffering" (Heb. 2:9, 10). And Peter, speaking to servants, says, "If you endure suffering even when you have done right, God will bless you for it. It was to this that God called you, for Christ himself suffered for you and left you an example, so that you would follow in his steps" (1 Pet. 2:20, 21).

These teachings may seem hard, but they seem so because we have wrong notions of human life. Too many of us imagine this life to be something valuable in itself, and religion something added to life to make it easier and more pleasant. We therefore embrace Christianity to the degree that it eases and comforts our lives.

Sufferings do not only cause us no real hurt, however; they actually promote our happiness and become the cause for real and solid joy. "Happy are you when people insult you and persecute you and tell all kinds of evil lies against you because you are my followers. Be happy and glad, for a great reward is kept for you in heaven" (Matt. 5:11, 12).

Christ does not try to comfort us in suffering by telling us how patience makes it easier to bear this hard state. He looks at it from another view, not as a situation needing comfort, but as a matter fit for congratulations. What strangers are we to Christ's spirit who reckon as a hardship what he recommends to us as a reason for rejoicing?

If suffering and self-denial make us more like Christ, they have done more for us than wealth can do. Whoever defends himself at the expense of losing Christ's attitude has done himself a far worse injury than his enemy did.

CHAPTER EIGHT
SELF-DENIAL

SELF-DENIAL is reasonable. Christian virtues are required because they are good and reasonable things to be done, not simply because God has the power to command what he pleases. If we are commanded to be humble, it is because humility is a suitable attitude for a dependent being.

If we are commanded to rejoice, it is at something truly joyful. If we are commanded to fear, it is to fear something truly dreadful. We are called to true attitudes as if being called to believe that two is half of four.

God does not lie. And God does not ask us to love things horrible or hate things lovely. God is perfectly reasonable. He therefore only wills that his reasonable creatures be more reasonable and perfect—more like himself. He will place on us no duties or attitudes unless they have this tendency. All his commands are for our own sakes and are really instructions in how to be happier than we would be without them.

We declare people insane when they imagine themselves to be something different from what they really are. We consider people fools who do not know the real value of things. An unbelieving sinner is thus insane and foolish;

he does not recognize what he is and he mistakes the value of things. Christianity is our education. It teaches us who we are and the true value of everything.

Some people, either through self-love or confusion, imagine themselves to be particularly in God's favor. They imagine their worldly success to be evidence of God's special blessing. But success in this life is hardly a mark of God's favor. "The Lord corrects everyone he loves, and punishes everyone he accepts as a son" (Heb. 12:6). The successful people who do not understand this verse are far from understanding the necessity for humility and self-denial. These people do not understand that humility is a more reasonable attitude than the belief that God always showers his children with worldly success.

All Christian duties and attitudes are ultimately reasonable. For instance, humility is simply a correct judgment of ourselves. To think worse of ourselves than we really are is no more of a virtue than pretending five to be less than four. To think better of ourselves than we really are is equally foolish.

Why is self-denial reasonable? Suppose that for some reason a lady has to walk on a rope high above a raging river. She is told while walking to deny herself the distraction of looking around at the beautiful waves. She is not to dress in fancy high heels or fish for trout during her walk. Would she feel these restrictions to be a hardship? Wouldn't denying herself be a reasonable thing?

"The gate to life is narrow, and the way that leads to it is hard," Jesus said (Matt. 7:14). If Christians are to walk on a narrow way, it behooves us to deny ourselves things that might lead us to fall. If we think self-indulgence is consistent with trying to keep on that narrow way, we might as reasonably think the lady on the rope could wear heels or fish for trout.

This is the foundation of Christian self-denial: In order to gain virtues, we try to avoid distractions. A person who wants to be healthy doesn't just take medicine; he avoids things that might make him sick.

One example of overindulgence is the sin of overeating, called gluttony. Gluttony is often difficult to define. However, a person who admits he has eaten so much Sunday dinner that he does not feel like doing anything except taking a nap—that person has spoken against himself.

Some people think gluttony means you have to eat yourself sick. But Scripture has a surer guide: "Whatever you do, whether you eat or drink, do it all for God's glory" (1 Cor. 10:31). A person who stuffs himself wants only to be idle, not to glorify God.

Christ spoke of how to fast at the same time he told how to pray and give alms. "When you go without food, wash your face and comb your hair, so that others cannot know that you are fasting—only your Father, who is unseen, will know. And your Father, who sees what you do in private, will reward you" (Matt. 6:17, 18). The same instruction and the same reasons are given for fasting as for almsgiving and private prayer.

Some people object that fasting is not a duty for all time. If by fasting they mean complete abstinence from food for a given period, I would agree. But I understand fasting to be abstinence from harmful, improper, excessive food, and thus appropriate for today.

Paul said, "I harden my body with blows and bring it under complete control, to keep myself from being disqualified after having called others to the contest" (1 Cor. 9:27). He was not undergoing self-denial to receive more spiritual gifts, but for the sake of his salvation. This mighty apostle thought his other virtues insecure without self-control.

CHAPTER NINE
NATURAL CORRUPTION

TWO truths stand out in the Scriptures: the general corruption of human nature and the absolute necessity of divine grace. Our corruption is like an illness. Either we are applying medicine (grace) to it and weakening it, or else by ignoring it we let it grow stronger.

We can thus evaluate our spiritual health. If we are denying ourselves, we are becoming stronger. But if we are in a state of self-love, we are not.

Sometimes when we speak of self-denial, we are thinking only of the obvious, sensual sins. But the most difficult sins to watch against are those of the spirit, such as self-love and pride. If we deny ourselves in some areas but indulge ourselves in others, we will be a curious and futile mixture. We must lay the axe to the root of the tree, denying not only individual pleasures but our whole indulgent natures, giving ourselves up to the Spirit of God.

Suppose Christianity required us to forget the language that we had grown up with and to learn to speak only a difficult new language. Could we possibly forget our natural language any other way than refusing to ever let ourselves speak it? Could we forget it by only using it occasionally? Wouldn't we have to keep, not only from speaking in it, but from reading, writing, and even thinking in it?

This can teach us the necessity of universal self-denial. Though Christianity does not command us to part with an old language, it does command us to part with an old nature and live in a new spirit. To get rid of the old nature, we must not only stop acting by it, but even liking, disliking, thinking, and wishing by it.

An examination of human nature and Christian nature convinces us that self-denial of the old nature is the beginning of virtue. Christianity teaches us three main principles. First, God is our only good, and we cannot be happy except in him. Second, our souls are immortal spirits, here on trial. Third, we must all appear before God's judgment seat to receive a sentence of eternal life or eternal death.

Every Christian is to live according to these principles, judging and thinking, choosing and avoiding, hoping and fearing, hating and loving according to them. We live as creatures sent here to prepare to live with God in everlasting happiness.

This makes all of Christianity a self-denial, a contradiction to our natural ideas. What could be more contradictory to our habitual notions than happiness in God alone? It is a happiness which our senses, those familiar guides, can neither see, hear, nor taste.

Look at natural man. He acts as if the world contained infinite varieties of happiness. He has a thousand pleasures and a thousand irritations, which show he thinks happiness can be found everywhere. For who gets irritated unless he thinks he has been cheated of some happiness? So Christianity is an obvious self-denial; it leads us from the enjoyments our senses have labeled happiness to a good our senses cannot perceive.

Our senses can tell us when to sleep, how close to get to a fire, and how much we can carry; they are proper guides in these things. But if we consult them regarding guilt, happiness, and excellence, it is like trying to hear with eyes or see with ears. Concerning the value of things, adults have the same judgment as children. We laugh at children's wishes for small trifles, but we fill our own thoughts with large trifles. When an adult thinks how happy he would be if he could just win a lottery or sweepstakes, that is just like the child who wishes he had enough money to buy twenty sticks of candy.

A person who has filled his mind with alcohol cannot think reasonably. One might as well not attempt a serious conversation with him. And a person who has filled his mind with sports, or fashion, or gossip, cannot think reasonably from a Christian point of view. He fails to perceive the pleasures of spiritual conversation.

CHAPTER TEN
THE HOLY SPIRIT

THE Holy Spirit makes us want to do good and enables us to do it.

Our natural lives are preserved by God, but we can't perceive his life-sustaining influence. The same is true of the Holy Spirit for our spiritual life. Jesus said, "The wind blows wherever it wishes; you hear the sound it makes, but you do not know where it comes from or where it is going. It is like that with everyone who is born of the Spirit" (John 3:8). We can feel the Holy Spirit's effects, as we can see the wind's effects; but we can't tell how he comes upon us.

According to Paul, "Those who are led by God's Spirit are God's sons" (Rom. 8:14). This shows that we must cooperate with the Holy Spirit. Rocks will not allow seeds to grow, and stony hearts will not bring forth the fruits of the Holy Spirit.

Everyone acknowledges that drunks and criminals cannot produce spiritual fruit. But neither can a mind busy with worldly cares. Why are little children incapable of Spirit-filled Christianity? It is not because they are drunks and criminals, but simply that their minds are always occupied with trifles. If as adults we have merely exchanged mental playthings, we can hardly expect sustained spiritual growth.

Philip goes to church and reads the Bible, but he doesn't get much out of it because his head is full of politics. He gets so irritated with his senators and representatives that he makes no effort to examine himself. His thoughts continually dwell on elections and legislation. Eugenia is the same way about business, and Sam is the same way about sports. It is not just gross sins, but any succession of worldly thoughts that can keep us from having time to listen to the Holy Spirit.

If you attempt to talk with a dying man about sports or business, he is no longer interested. He now sees other things as more important. People who are dying recognize what we often forget, that we are standing on the brink of another world.

The Holy Spirit is working in our hearts to give us a new understanding. To the extent that we nourish old passions, we resist the Holy Spirit. We make ourselves less likely to delight in his inspirations. We must be free of false hopes to rejoice in the Spirit's comforts.

A man may go hear comedians and laugh at their jokes, but if he is peevish and grouchy the rest of the time, no one would call him good-humored. And if we are very devout in church, but frivolous away from church, we can hardly be called Christians. If a greedy person prays generous prayers, he is still greedy. And if a person is reverent in a daily prayer but never thinks of God any other time, he is not a Christian.

People talk as they think. Sports fans, in normal conversation, say, "You've thrown me a curve there" and "I'll have to punt my way out of this situation." Television fans use the phrases of their favorite characters. And committed

Christians will find their speech punctuated with references to Christ. They will talk with like-minded people about the same subjects whether at church or in homes.

When a pastor preaches, people consider him to be simply doing his job. All preachers preach, but if he is as edifying in normal speech as in the pulpit, people will take more notice of the sermons. What he says through the week will add weight to what he says on Sunday. Conversely, a pastor who always trifles in conversation lessens his power of influencing his hearers.

Parents occasionally try to advise a son or daughter about the importance of Christianity. This will do the child good if he hears his parents speak highly of Christianity—and act it out—at other times. But if they only praise Christianity when they are advising him to follow it, he thinks they are only doing a parental duty, much like providing food and clothes.

A mother teaches her daughter Bible stories. The daughter likes the Bible stories, but notices that Mommy, in her own reading, is most interested in romances and homemaking magazines. The daughter is educated by what the mother does. Our conversation and ordinary life affect the people living around us. We will either let them harden in sin or we will alert them to Christianity.

CHAPTER ELEVEN
TRASHY READING

READING on wise and virtuous subjects is, next to prayer, the best improvement of our hearts. It enlightens us, calms us, collects our thoughts, and prompts us to better efforts. We say that a man is known by the friends he keeps; but a man is known even better by his books.

It is reckoned dangerous not to guard our eyes; it is even more dangerous not to guard our reading. What we read enters more deeply than what we happen to see. Reading is to our souls what food is to our bodies; we can do ourselves much good or much harm by our choices.

You might think it dull to read Christian books. But when you come to find in God your only happiness, you will think Christian books the most exciting. To a Spirit-filled person, Christian books are a feast and joy for the mind.

But trashy novels and romances! If you have spare time, use it for taking a nap or playing mumblety-peg instead. They'll do you less harm than reading trash.

And after all, where did we come up with this concept of "spare time," anyway? Is there any time for which we aren't accountable to God? Is there any time during which

God doesn't care what you are doing? *No Christian has ever had spare time.* You may have spare time from labor or necessity, you may stop working and refresh yourself, but no Christian ever had time off from living like a Christian.

You have time to recreate and refresh yourself, but that time is to be governed by Christian wisdom. Many people are doomed to such hardship that they can rarely choose what they want to do. But if you have "spare time," you have the power to choose the best things, the best ways of life, opportunities for self-improvement.

A scriptural teaching that seems quite reasonable is, "Much is required from the person to whom much is given" (Luke 12:48). A life with leisure time affords great opportunities. Had you been born in a different time as a servant or slave, especially under a cruel master, you would have been doing God's work simply by dedicating your daily toil to God. Being free of that burden, you should look on yourself as God's servant, spending your time laboring after his desires. You have no more time of your own than a slave; but your Master gives you freedom to choose your means of service.

CHAPTER TWELVE
SOAP OPERAS AND PAJAMA COMEDIES

CAN a Christian watch soap operas and pajama comedies? Absolutely not, in my opinion. We would think it strange if a person who doesn't swear visits buildings simply to hear curses. It's equally ridiculous for modest men and women to sit and watch other men and women act immodestly. Non-Christians are understandably delighted with sexual wordplay, because they tell sexual jokes themselves. But for Christians who never tell sexual jokes to laugh at them on TV contradicts common sense.

When you see actors playing the parts of prostitutes and adulterers, do you believe them to be committed to Christ? Hardly. If an actor's part approves and encourages immodesty, that's as sinful as encouraging theft.

NOTE: During Law's early life, the most popular stage plays were witty sexual farces with double entendres, closet lovers, and other forms of titillation. The closest modern equivalent would be television's "pajama comedies." (*Three's Company* is a familiar recent example.) Since Law's ire is directed toward sexual titillation in drama, this edition of his book refers to pajama comedies and soap operas to make his point. The chapter's concluding couplet originally appeared in an eighteenth-century magazine (*The Spectator*, Number 79) and has been modernized for this edition.

What is modesty? Is it outside behavior or an inward attitude? If modesty is only outside behavior, then I can see how a person who acts modestly himself could delight in others' immodesty. But I can't comprehend how a person who wants every thought pure would seek out soap operas or even remain in the room while they're on.

Do not misunderstand me. When I say a pajama comedy is immodest, I do not mean every person who watches a pajama comedy is also immodest. (I think astrology makes no sense, but that doesn't mean every believer in astrology has no sense.) The way we have been raised may influence us to do something that does not fit our general principles. But, as I already said, I cannot understand how a person seeking to live a holy life could waste time watching soap operas or other sex-saturated programs.

I once heard a woman excuse herself about watching soap operas by saying she only watched them with her family. "I still go to church and read my Bible," she said. "Soap operas don't cut into my time too much. They never interfere with my daily devotions."

That hardly comes to the point. A good many wicked things could be done without cutting into her "quiet times." The question is how these shows affect her attitudes. Does her watching accord with God's will, and is it appropriate for one led by the spirit of Christ? If so, she could watch the show with her family or without. If not, then it certainly doesn't make the situation better to have her family watch with her. We do not make a bad thing right by calling it "family time." This lady would hardly tell her pastor, "I occasionally get drunk, but only with my family."

If watching soap operas is a harmless and useful means of recreation, like walking, bike-riding, exercise, or good conversation, the lady need not excuse herself at all. If it's bad, then it hardly helps that she does it rarely. We would laugh at someone who said, "I occasionally commit adultery, but I still go to church and read my Bible. Adultery doesn't cut into my time too much. It never interferes with my daily devotions."

Suppose you had never seen a soap opera before. You are a Christian and want to evaluate it by scriptural principles. So first you ask what a soap opera is. You are told it is a performance in which actors try to move viewers emotionally with dialogues and action. The scripts (you are told) are written by intelligent, imaginative writers. These scripts primarily describe imaginary intrigues and love scenes. The dialogues center on lust and passion. They are performed by actors trained to present lustful passion in an appealing way.

You would not, in your Bible, find a commandment specifically against this activity. But you would certainly judge it to be out of keeping with the nature of Christianity.

True indeed were the gentleman's words:

> Her right eye views the Word, her left the soaps;
> She gives both God and Satan equal hopes.

CHAPTER THIRTEEN
REAL CHRISTIANITY

SO many people tend to confuse religious devotion and religious emotion. Consider a woman at a Christian concert. She is (to her mind) joyful in God's praise and fervent in worship. But her fervor may be due more to the intensity of the music than to true worship. An emotional high does not necessarily constitute genuine devotion to God.

Nor is the search for correctness in Christian belief necessarily a sign of the person's zeal for God. John is very concerned for correct doctrine. He is always eager to read books and pamphlets against cults and other denominations. There is only one type of religious book he doesn't care for, and that is anything on personal devotion. He has no keen interest in books on humility, love, heavenly-mindedness, self-denial, or kindness.

Many people are like John in this respect. They always want more instruction *on certain points.* They will read certain books, but they can't bear to be instructed about any matter in which they are possibly mistaken, to their spiritual detriment. They are grateful if you tell them the dates that the Gospels were written. They are thankful for you explaining the words *rabboni* or *Anathema Maranatha.*

They are glad for such "useful" instruction. But if you touch upon matters that really concern them, these religious people, so fond of religious truth, cannot bear to be instructed.

Alas, so many intelligent people become preoccupied with dates and linguistic problems concerning the Bible that they have no time to seriously consider the Bible's main theme, God's love for us and our loving response to him. They seem so concerned for truth, yet neglect the real purpose of truth, which is to bring us closer to the God of truth.

Why do we consult lawyers? Is it to hear lectures on legal codes? To hear about legal disputes? No, indeed, we consult them because we want assistance on our own case. To further that end, we give them all the information we can.

Why do we go to doctors? To learn about medical history? To hear of other people's diseases? No, we want a cure for our own. And we are glad for them to examine every part of our lives, even how we eat and sleep.

Why do we act this way toward doctors and lawyers? Because we're serious about the matter. And when we are serious about Christianity, we are equally glad to have our lives examined. Serious Christians are more concerned with rooting out sin and growing in grace than in maintaining an emotional high or resolving all the scholarly questions about Christian doctrine. So we read the books and consult the people who are most effective in finding corruption and leading to health. If we don't act this way, if we try to cover up what we think and say and do, we are not serious about moving toward Christian perfection.

CHAPTER FOURTEEN
PRAYER

OUR Savior is now at the right hand of God, interceding for us. Knowing this should encourage our prayers. When we pray, we are doing on earth what Christ is perpetually doing for us in heaven. Since our prayers are only acceptable to God through the merits of Jesus Christ, we pray to God in the most prevailing way when we remember Christ's name and his merits.

Devotion may be considered either as voiced prayers, public and private, or as an attitude of the heart. External devotion only has value when it proceeds from internal devotion. When Christians are asked to pray without ceasing, this refers to the inward state; we cannot be every moment voicing prayers. In the same way we confess our faith only at certain times, but the faith stays with us always.

The reason for prayer is found in God's nature and our nature. God is the sole fountain of happiness; humans are weak and full of needs. Prayer, then, is an application or ascent of the heart to God as the cause of all happiness. The person who prays most fervently is the one who most realizes both his weakness and God's power to relieve sorrow. To be filled with a prayerful spirit, we must know ourselves. When we lose track of our own littleness or of God's greatness, or when we think pleasure can be found anywhere besides God, we lose our state of devotion. We can only desire what we feel we need. If we feel less needy, then, we become less fervent for God's relief.

Sometimes we tell people to be more fervent in prayer. That does as much good as telling people to be happy or sad. People wear their attitudes based on their evaluations of circumstances. If they perceive things to be going well, they will be happy; if they perceive things to be going poorly, they will be sad; if they perceive their lives to be empty, they will be fervent in prayer. A person generally does not grieve when life goes well; he doesn't rejoice when life goes poorly; and he doesn't long for God when he is satisfied with life.

Suppose you were to call a man away from a sumptuous feast. You tell him to go into the next room and be hungry for a half-hour; then he can go back to feasting. You tell him he must really feel this hunger deeply.

He might obey you by going into the hunger room. He might even sit there licking his lips for a half-hour. But the man is not really hungry. Why not? Because he has just come from a feast, and he is returning to a feast, and that dulls one's appetite.

This is the position of a great many Christians. They are always at a feast—a feast of pleasure and satisfaction. Then they go to Scripture and are told to hunger after God as their only real satisfaction. But their appetite is already dulled. If any person is perplexed to find himself not often hungering for God, he should explore the likely reason: he is already full.

Many people would like to pray fervently, so they read books on prayer and try to be more emotional. But they haven't taken the only possible way to become more fervent: altering their lives, which must involve our refusal to treasure worldly pleasures. We cannot live one way and pray another. It is like a woman expecting to become athletic by reading sports books and wishing she were so.

When Julia prays, she confesses herself to be a sinner. She repeats the words of Scripture, "I know that good does not live in me—that is, in my human nature" (Rom. 7:18). Yet Julia cannot bear to be informed of any imperfection. Could there be a stronger proof that Julia's prayers are insincere? If a woman were to admit to being lame, she would not be angry with those who offered her assistance.

Religious devotion means what it sounds like—being devoted to God. A devoted soul constantly rises toward God with habits of love, trust, hope, and joy. Actually, a person is not so much exhorted as carried into devotion. Consider these enlivening texts:

"But we know that when Christ appears, we shall be like him, for we shall see him as he really is" (1 John 3:2).

"Just as we wear the likeness of the man made of earth, so we will wear the likeness of the Man from heaven" (1 Cor. 15:49).

"Let us give thanks to the God and Father of our Lord Jesus Christ! Because of his great mercy he gave us new life by raising Jesus Christ from death" (1 Pet. 1:3).

"He will change our weak mortal bodies and make them like his own glorious body, using that power by which he is able to bring all things under his rule" (Phil. 3:21).

These truths shine a light on the soul that will kindle it into flames of love for God. The way to live in devotion is to contemplate these thoughts continually. They will enable our little anxieties and selfish desires to be swallowed up in one great desire of future glory.

This type of devotion is in Scripture called living by faith and not by sight (2 Cor. 5:7). The invisible things of the future life determine our desires. This devotion makes us eager to pray; and our prayers in turn enliven our devotion.

People who like music want to go to concerts, and the concerts give them a greater appreciation for the music. People who desire to be with God pray, and prayer increases their delight in God. We can judge the sincerity of our prayers by our daily attitudes; we can judge our daily attitude by our fervency in prayer.

Some people think we need only pray for short periods of time. But continuance in prayer is stressed nearly as often in Scripture as prayer itself. Jesus gave the parable of the unjust judge to "teach them [the disciples] that they should always pray and never become discouraged" (Luke 18:1). Paul does not just command us to pray, but to "pray at all times" (1 Thess. 5:17). And in Colossians 4:2, the same apostle says, "Be persistent in prayer."

No one can specify how long a person ought to pray. But a person whose daily prayer lasts fifteen minutes or less has a definite disadvantage. The cares and distractions of life make us all more or less unprepared for devotion. If our time of prayer is short, we end our prayers before our devotion has really begun. It often takes several minutes to collect our minds and turn our hearts to the business at hand. A longer time for prayer gives the heart leisure to fall away from worldly concerns and exercises the mind.

All of us are inconstant in our prayers. We heartily attend some spiritual thoughts; our minds wander away from others. It is therefore common sense to extend our prayer times, to give our wandering minds an opportunity to rejoin us. A person who always prays for a short time, in a hurry, may pray his whole life without experiencing real devotion. If a person were to think, before beginning to pray, what prayer is, what he's praying for, and to whom he's praying, he would gain a more devout mind. I do not intend this, or anything else, as a specific rule for an effective prayer. This is only to show that there are ways to assist our devotion.

There are two seasons of our hearts when we can particularly learn about ourselves and how to foster our devotional lives: the times when we are most involved in prayer and the times when we least want to pray. Think about what happened the last time you had a really effective period of prayer. What circumstances were you in? What had you been doing? What were your thoughts? If you find out what made that prayer time so effective, you may be able to raise your devotion at other times. If you write down for occasional review things that stimulate your prayer time, you will find your efforts well rewarded.

And, from the other side, think about the last time your prayers were hindered. What thoughts were in your head? What had you done or intended to do? What emotions were you feeling? If you can figure out what hindered your prayers, you can make efforts to avoid it. If certain thoughts or subjects distract your mind from prayer, you have information on how to alter your life. Things that lower our minds will be daily guarded against by those who want to be daily alive to God.

Frequent and prolonged prayer aids in spiritual improvement. In praying we renew our convictions, enlighten our minds, and fortify our hearts. The benefit of prayer is not only that God hears it, but that it alters us. Some people argue for short prayers by observing that God does not need to hear our lives discussed at length. True enough, God doesn't; but *we* do. It does not take much prayer to move God, but it takes a great deal to move us.

If God does not give us something at the first asking, if he waits until later, it is not because our prayers have made any change in God. But prayer makes a change in ourselves, for it renders us ready for God's grace.

Prayer is most effective when we specify our needs and imperfections. Of course God does not need to be informed of them, but it informs us. We see ourselves more truly. When we detail all our circumstances and thoughts, we are making a mirror for our lives; God's light shines on the mirror and lets us see ourselves.

Don't contentedly confess yourself a sinner in general; this only shows you to be a human being, for we are all sinners. Lay open your sins specifically. Seeing them in God's light will influence you to amend your life. And don't just pray for "grace to be better," but ask the Holy Spirit to aid you in those specific areas you most lack.

Being specific puts truth in our prayers. A person might think he really wants humility if he asks for it in general terms. But if he begins asking for grace to be humble in a variety of specific situations, he may discover himself not to be so eager for it after all. If he were in prayer to look to instances of people being poor in spirit, he may find he doesn't have a real desire to be like that. The only way to know if our hearts are true when we pray for virtues is to ask for them regarding specific situations.

If a greedy man were to beg God daily to frustrate his attempts to become wealthier, one of two things would happen: the greed would win and he would cease praying, or the prayers would win and he would cease being greedy. He could hardly continue in greed if every day he listed his money-making schemes, one by one, and asked God to topple them.

Anyone may grow spiritually from prayer if he earnestly desires to. Most people do not appear to know themselves;

but we may know ourselves by presenting our lives to God in prayer.

Let me add one word more: The person who learns to really pray learns the greatest secret of a holy and happy life. God is suited to our natures. He is equal to our needs, a constant source of comfort and refreshment. He will fill us with peace and joyful expectations here and eternal happiness hereafter. The man whose heart is full of God lives at the top of human happiness. He is furthest removed from those disturbances that vex the minds of worldly men.

CHAPTER FIFTEEN
IMITATING JESUS CHRIST

"JUST as we wear the likeness of the man made of earth, so we will wear the likeness of the Man from heaven" (1 Cor. 15:49). Since Christianity intends us to be like Jesus in the afterlife, it is no wonder we are expected to be like Jesus in this life.

We are called to imitate Christ. This does not mean performing all of his exact actions, but having his attitudes. Just as no doctrines are Christian unless they fit Christ's teaching, no life is Christian unless it fits Christ's pattern.

Jesus said, "I am the way, the truth, and the life; no one goes to the Father except by me" (John 14:6). Many Christians think they have fulfilled these words simply by believing in Jesus Christ. But as we must believe in his truth and receive from him life, we must follow his way.

Jesus Christ came into the world to save the world. Salvation should also be our greatest concern, both for ourselves and others. Of course, we cannot contribute toward salvation what Jesus did. The work of salvation is carried on in a variety of ways. For an unlearned person to desire instruction may promote salvation as truly as for a teacher to instruct. That teachable attitude may draw others into learning as effectively as the teacher's ability. Often a teacher's success is due more to the people being taught than to his own strength. Any of us, no matter what our level of learning, can exemplify holiness and make our lives a lesson.

Christ is the Savior of the world. To be like him, we must attempt to save others (although, as I said, we cannot save in the sense that he did). Paul said, "How can you be sure, Christian wife, that you will not save your husband? Or how can you be sure, Christian husband, that you will not save your wife?" (1 Cor. 7:16). Paul clearly thinks it a possibility that we can have a share in our spouse's salvation. If this is true about a spouse, why not another relative, a friend, a neighbor?

Troy is a devout Christian who always tries to be around other devout Christians. He avoids being with unbelievers whenever possible. Troy has failed to realize that this is like a doctor avoiding sick people. We cannot be dutiful Christians if our concern for our own purity makes us neglect our duty to witness to unbelievers. All of us are hired to work in Christ's vineyard.

Claude has his head full of future Christianity. He often thinks what he would do if he were extremely rich. He would not spend it all on himself, like other millionaires, but would give huge portions to charitable causes.

Claude presently has a middle-class income. He spends it the way other middle-class people do. He doesn't limit his comfort, but continually talks about how he would limit his spending if he were rich. Come to your senses, Claude! Do not talk about what you'd do if you were an angel instead of a man or a millionaire instead of middle-class. Do now what you would want to do if you were wealthy; deny yourself and be charitable.

Fred is a Christian businessman whose desire to do

great things for God makes him overlook the little good things that are in his power. Fred often thinks how perfect life would be if he were a pastor; then he'd spend all his time caring for God and other people.

Don't believe it, Fred! Why do you think you would spread the spirit of Christianity throughout a church when you aren't doing it in your own family? What about the people who work for you? If they do their jobs well, you never trouble your head about their Christianity. You open your restaurant before noon on Sundays, never asking your employees if this causes them to miss church. You think that as a clergyman you would lay down your life for the flock, yet you won't lay aside part of the Sunday dinner business for your employees. You're not called to be a martyr, Fred; you're only called to give up some profit to let your employees worship if they wish to do so.

Jeannie is a good young lady with high ideals. She intends, if she ever gets married and has a family, to be the most devout wife and mother ever. Her house will be a regular school of religion; her children will grow up surrounded with the presence of God. Jeannie really believes she intends this.

Well, Jeannie, you do not know whether you will have a family. But you have yourself right now. You think you will read Bible stories to your children; how often do *you* read the Bible now? You think you will pray with your little ones every day; how much do you pray now? You think your family's conversation will be filled with God; how much are your thoughts centered on God now? Changing your state from singleness to wife and mother will not alter your spiritual way of life.

People always please themselves with an imaginary perfection to be arrived at when their circumstances are better.

"I have come down from heaven," Jesus said, "to do

not my own will but the will of him who sent me" (John 6:38). Was Jesus a loser by neglecting human happiness and devoting himself to God's will? Can we be losers by devoting ourselves to God alone?

One further observation about imitating Christ. Nothing is more likely to fill us with Christlike attitudes than reading the Gospels, which contain his life and conversations. We usually think we have read a book well enough when we know what it contains. With the Gospels, however, we are not just reading to know what they contain, but to fill our hearts with their spirit. By constantly spending time with our Lord, we shall find our hearts hungering and thirsting after righteousness.

CHAPTER SIXTEEN
PERFECTION

WE exhort people to a good many things: studying poetry, becoming rich or famous, learning to use computers. If someone were to ask me why he should learn to use a computer, I would tell how it could benefit his life. But if he were to ask me what good computer knowledge would do after his life ended, I wouldn't have an answer. Only Christianity can stand the trial of that second question.

Pyrrhus, the king of ancient Epirus, told his counselor, Cineas, that he intended to conquer all the nations around him. "Why?" asked Cineas. "What will we do then?"

"We will live without fear and enjoy ourselves and our friends," replied Pyrrhus.

"Then, sir," asked Cineas, "why don't we live without fear now?"

Suppose we were to ask a Christian what he will do when he gets the wealth or education or position he wants. He would probably say he intends to be close to God. Then why not be close to God now?

Only a true dedication of ourselves to Christianity can make it fully pleasant for us. When we are divided between God and the world, we don't have the pleasures of either.

We have enough Christianity to check our worldly enjoyments and interrupt our entertainments, but not enough to let us taste their satisfactions. We don't dare neglect Christianity; but we are as hesitant to pursue it fully as we are fearful to pursue the world fully. We are as unhappy as a slave who serves his master grudgingly but doesn't dare run away. The only reason many people can tolerate Christianity is because it doesn't take up much time.

Earl goes to church. He can't understand people who don't believe in God; he also can't understand people who live for God daily. Earl accepts religion because it seems like an easy way to please God. It doesn't take up much time and is such a decent thing to be involved with. But when Earl thinks of happiness or delight, he certainly doesn't think of religion. He continues for years in a practice that does him no real harm—or good.

Let me exhort you, if you're going to profess Christianity, to devote yourself wholly to God. You may then have the peace of a unified heart.

Christian perfection involves overcoming difficulties. You could not love your neighbors if you had no neighbors to love. And you could not attempt to overcome the world if it had no temptation. If all the people you knew were devout, humble, and heavenly minded, it would involve no overcoming to be like them. But to be humble among the proud and devout among the worldly takes effort. It is ridiculous to say we would be devoted to God if our position weren't so difficult; *every* position in this world is difficult.

We look at other believers in God, good churchgoing people, who live a "normal" life. We think God can't reject so many religious people, so we'll be safe if we're like them. We don't know in the case of any other churchgoer whether he is bound for heaven or hell. But when Christ has said, "But the gate to life is narrow, and the way that leads to it is hard, and there are few people who find it" (Matt. 7:14), it's foolish to complacently glide along with the majority. Alas, the majority of religious people are too much occupied with seeking earthly happiness.

Heavenly happiness is far more secure than earthly happiness. Bad luck or misfortune cannot keep us from heavenly happiness, nor malice by our enemies, nor betrayal by our friends. If our hearts remain true, neither life nor death, nor supernatural beings nor men, can separate us from the happiness of God.

SCRIPTURE INDEX